Ark of The Covenant On The Move

Written By

Rev. Dr. Derrick A. Hill

revdrderrickhill@gmail.com

Preface

This journey that we are about to take together will be one of grave importance. Many times it is hard to phantom the hidden revelation within the Word of God. Many topics and many principles, precepts and concepts are missed because of the nature of the teachers. Many times the church is so busy trying to get money or building something till we miss the basic concept of what Christ wanted us to do. If we teach and live the principles of the God then He will take care of His house. Each of us need the movement of the wisdom God in order to combat today's struggles.

This journey is very much needed because we need the depths of the word of God to face the adversary's attacks. This present stage of life movement is deeply believe that we are in the last days. If this is true we need the fortified word of God, the deep seeded standards that brought us through when we were in the loins. When need to unzip the past depths that the prophets and apostles laid before us and move from this new age revolution. In order to do this we have return to the beginning and work our way forward.

This particular book will take us from the beginning to the present day. This journey is very important because of the connection and truth from the old to the new. Many concepts and precepts are missed because of the connection. We need to see ourselves in the beginning so we can reveal the depths as we go along. This material is for a pealing back of the layers so each of us can recognize who we are and whom we belong. We need to see ourselves as we were meant to be in order to break the evolution of what we have become. As we move through this journey each of us will fine different levels that will reveal hidden truths about how we became and how we become.

We have to look forward to the revelation instead of man's inspiration that feed our emotions instead of building up our Spirit. With this particular material we will be able to see the fundamentals of being lifted by the truth or confused by the deception. So together we are going to walk through a spiritual uncovering that will not only help to renew our minds but strengthen our spirits. This particular material is nothing new but something that need to be delivered unto the people of God so we all can come on one accord about Christ Jesus. If we constantly feed our spirits then we can steadily move forward spiritually which will defeat the enemy physically. Together united we can create a strong front for the land of darkness to help another into the light.

This is not for me to say that I am some type of spiritual giant. I am a student of the Word of God. My attention is to give our people ammunition to fight the adversary with but also I want to give them truth and understanding. I also want to give the people of God information that can reveal and uncover nuggets that they can study for themselves and use before they make mistakes. So I offer what I have simply out of love and joy of the Word of God.

So come take this journey and remember "The Ark of the Covenant on the Move."

Chapter One

We are going to introduce the bases for this particular journey. We are going to start here but that does not mean that this is the beginning. Understand that we are starting here because we need to identify what we recognize so we can have a focus point. Now this focus point will run us in two different directions. In our direction we will see and understand the beginning to the present. Two things we must understand is that everything is pointing forward for us to stand on today,

Right now I know that this is a little strange to us but before this journey is over we will together get to a place and shout "Glory." So let us get started.......

The Ark of the Covenant is first mention in Exodus 25. It is recorded saying, "And they shall make an ark of shittim wood two cubits and a half shall be the length thereof, and a cubit and a half the breadth thereof, and a cubit and a half the height thereof. And thou shalt overlay it with pure gold, round about. And thou shalt cast four rings of gold for it, and put them in four corners thereof; and two rings shall be in the one side of it, and two rings in the other side of it. And thou shalt make staves of shittim wood and overlay them with gold. And thou shalt put the staves into the rings by the sides of the ark that the ark may be borne with them. The staves shall be in the rings of the ark: they shall not be taken from it. And thou shalt put into the ark the testimony which I shall give thee, And thou shalt make a mercy seat of pure gold: two cubits and a half shall be the length thereof, and a cubit and a half the breadth thereof, And thou shalt make two cherubim of gold of beaten work shalt thou make them, in the two ends of the mercy seat.

And make one cherub on the one end, and the other cherub on the other end: even of the mercy seat shall ye make the cherubims on the two ends thereof. And the cherubims shall stretch forth their wings on high, covering the mercy seat with their wings, and their faces shall look one to another; toward the mercy seat shall the faces of the cherubims be. And thou shalt put the mercy seat above upon; and in the ark thou shalt put the testimony that I give thee .And there I will meet with thee, and I will commune with thee from above the mercy seat, from between the two cherubims which are upon the ark of the testimony, of all things which I will give thee in commandment unto the children of Israel." (Exodus 25:10-22)

Now we want to take a look into the Ark of the Covenant piece by piece to uncover so fantastic truths. The first thing we are going to look at the history of the wood. This is important to see the special significance as it relates to then now and the future. Shittim wood" is said to signify "the merit of the Lord's righteousness," but before we undertake to explain what this means, we must consider what kind of wood is referred to. With a single exception we find the term "shittim wood" mentioned nowhere in the Sacred Scripture except in the books of Moses, and in connection with the tabernacle. The root meaning of the Hebrew word has never been discovered, and scholars differ widely in their views as to what kind of tree is meant.

The only other passage in which the term occurs is Isaiah 41:19, where we read, "I will plant in the wilderness the cedar of shittah, the myrtle, and the oil tree." In the Authorized Version of the English Bible this is translated, "I will plant in the wilderness the cedar, the shittah tree, and the myrtle, and the oil tree." Here the Hebrew pointing clearly indicates that a special kind of cedar is meant, and this meaning is in accord with the earliest Jewish tradition. It is recognized that "shittah" was a region, situated in the northern part of the Sinai Peninsula, and it is so marked in many of the maps of the Bible lands. We have concluded, therefore, that "shittim wood" was derived from a kind of cedar that, at the time of Moses, flourished in a certain part of the Sinai Peninsula.

Now today no such tree exists within the region and this causes a problem for some biblical scholars. It cause so much of a problem that they reworked their view to say that the Shittim Tree has to be a part of the acacia, a species of scrubby locust which grows in that general locality. Now with this view the scholars even re-figured the original text. Considering, then, that the identification of the shittim wood with cedar is not possible, the translators of the Scripture have been divided, some remaining true to the original pointing, and others separating the two words shittah and cedar as if they represented different species. Thus in the authorized version of the Septuagint and the Vulgate the above verse is translated, "I will plant in the wilderness the cedar, the shittah tree, the myrtle, and the oil tree." Some, however, clings to the original Scripture and defines shittim wood as "a wood of the most excellent cedar."

The view that is popular at present is based on the assumption that, because there is no trace of any species of cedar now growing on the Sinai Peninsula, we must conclude that none ever existed there. Yet it is well known that, due to various natural causes, the flora of any region may be radically changed by the hand of time. It is a notable fact that the famous cedars of Lebanon have almost disappeared from their historic locality. According to an eminent investigator, no more than a dozen species remained in the year 1890, and these were slowly dying.

It is quite probable that fifty years from now, lacking documentary evidence, men would conclude, according to the same arguments used by scholars with reference to shittim wood, that the temple of Solomon could not have been built of cedar wood because no source of that material was available. We have had a similar experience illustrating the total disappearance of a tree, in the immediate neighborhood of Philadelphia, where the chestnut tree has become entirely extinct within our own memory as a result of the chestnut blight. We have been unable to find conclusive evidence upon the subject, but from such study as we have been able to make of the topography of Sinai, especially in certain regions toward the northern part of that peninsula, there would appear to be no inherent reason why cedar trees should not at one time have been found there.

Furthermore I prefer to stick to the original writing and instead of trying to discard the Word of God I want to uncover the hidden truths. The scripture read, "And they shall make an ark of shittim wood;" (Exodus 25:10). Now if I figure in all the factors that this particular wood was in abundance at the time of Moses. In that I wanted to understand why our Lord out of all other trees would chose that particular tree. This was like a lightning bolt knocked me off my feet. Now Shittim wood" is said to signify "the merit of the Lord's righteousness," and this was very important. There is, for instance, no other tree growing in Sinai that attains a size sufficient to provide boards of the enormous dimensions specified for the tabernacle. The critics meet this objection by supposing that the Israelites were familiar with the art of joining. There is no evidence that they possessed this knowledge, and if this were the mode by which the tabernacle boards were to be constructed, it is almost unbelievable that directions with reference to it should not have been given in the Scripture, where we find so many detailed instructions with reference to other matters. We would contend, therefore, that the shittim wood mentioned is indeed the wood of "a most excellent cedar," distinguished in species from the "cedar of Lebanon," but a tree of the same family.

This interpretation is important in view of the spiritual significance given to the shittim wood in the writings, namely, "the Lord's merit and righteousness." It is clear from many passages in which cedars are mentioned that the signification here given has reference to the cedar tree.[3] By "the Lord's merit and righteousness" is meant that attitude of mind with reference to the formation of the spiritual church which is poetically expressed by the psalmist in the words, "Except the Lord build the house, they labor in vain that build it."[4] Only an attitude of deep humility can inspire anyone to seek Divine aid, and turn to the Word for instruction and guidance. Pride and the conceit of one's own intelligence turns man away from the Word, and closes his mind against the influence of the heavens. Religion then loses its saving power, and when this happens in all parts of the world the Lord must come to re-establish the spirit of humility, and restore a living faith. This is why it is said in the Writings: "Except the Lord had come into the world, no flesh could have been saved."

So I had to ask myself how this connect throughout the Word of God. "Except the Lord build the house, they labor in vain that build it" was the key for me. Through this perverse time man has come to believe that they are God. They are growing children in test tubes as well as having same sex marriages. In that they are throwing mockery to our Lord by exploiting such vile interpretation saying that we can bring a child into any situation. In conducting such action it is easy to see that man's derogation is a pulling away from God. A delusion has spread across the sight of man and they try to distort the true essence of God's word so we cannot reach out potential as well as produce the power that we have access to. In order to understand how this fit I have to show you something that is in the beginning.

The Shittim wood was used to form the Ark of the Covenant. The Lord's merit and righteousness is the definition. In the beginning the Bible records, "And the Lord God formed man of the dust of the ground," (Genesis 2:7) God took the dust of the earth and formed man, this form was basically the "waste" of the earth. This is very powerful because it cannot be confused that the form that man was made out of had no significance physically. Physically it was the waste spiritually it was the supporting factor to the old. Understand that the waste had no primarily function until God formed it. But once He formed it there still was nothing but a form. God being God knew our actions before the beginning of recorded time so this was a powerful demonstration of the old connecting to the new.

In order for the form to be effective it took the Lord breathing into the nostrils of the form to make it a living soul. God had done something so in response man had to do something to remain in favor of the Lord. This is significant because it man doing something that took them out of favor of the Lord. So man had rituals that had to be perform and sacrifices that had to be done and when the law was introduce man was set up for the coming of the new. God's form of waste became something a living soul and that soul became tainted. In the beginning man was recognize throughout all creation as having dominion. It wasn't how they were created but how they were connected to the Lord. The waste became perfect because the waste was clean. Many times when we think of waste we refer it to garbage or nasty. But in God's wisdom knowing that whatever is taken through Him is clean. So waste became clean and perfect like it was recycle through the perfect communion of the triune.

When the Lord commission the children of Israel to build the Ark of the Covenant we see that the Lord was issuing a new thing. Man had gotten so vile that God had to destroy it all except a small band and a few animals. From that point God unveiled a plan that was impossible to understand then and miraculous to us now. God brought forth a nation from bondage of a count of seventy. From a count of seventy most scholars disagree on the exact number but I believe it was a million plus came forth and represented the baptism of the Holy Ghost. From that point on God begin to reveal a new thing and it form was Christ in us as He blew in the nostrils and the form became a living soul.

The Shittim wood is the Lord's merit and righteousness and the Jews were well aware of this. So God was building something that was formed by His merit and righteousness because man at the present has none. God was forming something that spoke out it is nothing that you have done or nothing that you can do it is all about God's merit and God's righteousness. You see God was speaking in a threefold statement saying that in the past you were not good enough now you cannot do enough but with my merit and righteousness you will be perfect again. So when our Lord spoke and commission them to build the Ark of the Covenant He was creating a model of me and you today.

Today we know that if we are a member of the Body of Christ then our form our house our body is a new creature. We are being transformed from inwardly out but our complete transform will not take place until we receive our heavenly form. Where our form of waste, nothing is changed from destructible to indestructible. The representation of our form was demonstrated from day one perfect. As we move through our journey when the Father looks upon us He sees His merit and righteousness not our filth and stains. It is because of the Lord Jesus Christ that we have been washed and cleansed again. From waste to perfection through Jesus Christ our Lord. So as our Lord command our brothers to build the ark He was telling them that there is something new about to happen and look no longer by what you do but by my merit and righteousness of my Son, Jesus Christ.

We must understand that at that point God was releasing a physical conformation for a spiritual revelation. If we look back we will see that our Lord is particular in the way of introducing a physical manifestation to a spiritual release that will have a powerful impact. From the beginning our Lord open up a masterful plan to bring back that which was perfect out of nothing, stain and brought back to perfection. Let us realize that this move was planned before the listing of recorded time. Our Lord has hidden significant markers for His people to fine that will release a wave of spiritual keys that will strengthen one in every battle from the adversary attacks. Remember He first speak, release, reveal and then manifest. Let us unlock this and see the miraculous master plan.

When man fell and God call out to Adam He was hidden. This was two-fold because Adam action represent a spiritual revelation. I am going to take it one step at a time because this is our base. The Bible says, "And the LORD God called unto Adam, and said unto him, Where art thou? And he said, I heard thy voice in the garden, and I was afraid because I was naked; and I hid myself." (Genesis 3:9-10) Now many read over words instead of uncovering the words to see its true understanding. The word "fear" means in Hebrew, "The root meaning of the word yara is "to flow" and is related to words meaning rain or stream as a flowing of water. In Hebrew thought fear can be what is felt when in danger or what is felt when in the presence of an awesome sight or person of great authority. These feelings flow out of the person in such as actions as shaking when in fear or bowing down in awe of one in authority.

Let us look at the word "naked," There are two main families of Hebrew words for naked or nakedness used. They are tackled in turn below with references and other information. In summary, the usage in the Garden is from the word-family based on *'ûwr*, where nakedness is seen as a state of being, possibly needing help to resolve, but not with a strong sense of condemnation or shame. Other uses of the Genesis 3 word (*'êrôm*) have the connotation of abandonment or helplessness. The other main word-family, where the noun forms have a much more definite sense of shame attached, are largely used by the prophets. The main use in the Pentateuch is in the legal passages, not narrative, with the exception of Noah's drunkenness. Interestingly, the verb form of this second family need not have a shameful connotation, but can have an ethically neutral sense (emptying something) or even a positive sense (the Spirit being poured out).

There is an interesting transition from Genesis 2 to 3. In Gen 2 (translated "They were naked and felt no shame"), the word used suggests a simple descriptive state of nakedness. In Gen 3 ("They were naked and sewed leaves ... they were naked and hid ... who told you, you were naked") there is still an essentially descriptive usage, but with the added connotation of being poor and destitute, and in need of help. It is important to note that at this point there is not the added significance of shame attached which comes later, in situations of deliberate or reckless actions. The first of these is seen with Noah's drunkenness, then (other than legal passages in the Pentateuch) the main use is in the prophetic writings.

Often here the use is as part of an extended metaphor image. But the earliest use, at the Fall, does not have the connotation of shame so much as of poverty and destitution.

Now as we release the uncovering let us see if we can gather the spiritual movement. When God called out to Adam, he responded I heard you Lord but I was afraid. For some they stop right there but let us go a little deeper. Adam responded I heard you Lord but there have been a release of flowing emotions and I did not know if I should stay away or come. In that sense the definition of his action was simple, "I cannot handle this." In Adams perfect state he was untainted with emotional baggage. He understood love, placement, and dominion. In those three attachment to his person he was perfect in his living, relationship, and work. That gave him, Adam a stand that position Him righteously in the presence of our Lord.

His love for what God had created for him was significance in the love that he had for the Lord. He recognized and realized that God was the creator of all and for that Adam love Him for being exactly who He was. Next Adam realized the love that God had for Him because God returned His love by meeting every need that Adam would possibly ever having including the physical. He understood his placement because he represented dominion over all that his Lord had created. His relationship was perfect with his work and his Lord. He realized that Eve was created out of him and for him.

Now how do that relate to us today. In our life our attacks are design to disrupt our emotional stability to cause an overflow that sends us spiraling out of control. In that the adversary uses a threefold attack sight, touch and thought and not necessarily in that order. But all geared to do the same thing send a massive wave of emotion to cause a physical reaction. If we are able to stabilize our emotion then our physical reactions will stay in touch with our spiritual connection to the heavenly body. We have to realize that our connection is the exact thing that the adversary tries to disrupt and force a reaction. Many times within the attacks of the adversary there are hidden designs to strengthen us within the attacks for God's glory. (But that is a different book so let us continue.)

Then Adam release something that might have been over looked by us if we just look at the words. The word says, "And the LORD God called unto Adam, and said unto him, Where art thou? And he said, I heard thy voice in the garden, and I was afraid because I was naked; and I hid myself." The focus is on "I was naked" now this is interesting because if we understand that God focuses on the spiritual relevance that manifest through the physical. When Adam said he was naked what was he really saying. So the word "naked" referred to "word-family based on *'ûwr*, where nakedness is seen as a state of being, possibly needing help to resolve, but not with a strong sense of condemnation or shame have the connotation of abandonment or helplessness."

Now with the flow of emotions that have over taken Adam when he heard God call out to him the process of reaction took him to a place for which shame had nothing to do with it, but he felt something that was in the processing that was out of his understanding. If we think that Adam was shame because he was naked that only works if he had never been naked in the presence of God. He knew nothing else but being naked it is not like he saw anything clothed. Adam saw all the animals and they were not clothed and he never had clothing and Eve had no clothing so why would shame have anything to do with it. But Adam said, "I was naked" so what was Adam referring to. Here is a thought if the flow of emotions had taken hold of him then Adam had to realize that he was unable to stop it he was helpless against it.

Understand that Adam had lived this long with the sense of having dominion over everything that was in his surrounding and within himself. He had strength over the lion command over the bears as well as having control over the gorillas. It had not been recorded that

Adam had to get angry about anything or sick from anything. Adam had control over himself as well as dominion over everything till this point. The emotional flow that was breaking through in him took him to a place where he had no control as well as questioning his very own dominion. Adam felt secure in the beginning because he felt worthy of walking with God and talking to God because Adam knew no fear. True righteousness brings no condemnation because Adam had never disobeyed God before. Adam understood that something was released in him that had never been released before because he had done something that he had never did before.

His self-worth had been brought into question and his dominion had transformed into nakedness because of knowing right from wrong. You see in knowing right from wrong brings us into awareness of judging ones action and understanding "I have failed." Adam understood from that point he had done wrong and his righteousness had no longer existed. From that point Adam felt his covering leave him, that he had been strip of his righteousness. Everything that he was and everything that he knew is now in question because of his understanding of wrong.

This is what happen to us when we do wrong. We feel the strip of righteousness the abandonment of our connection. We are flood with an emotional attack that is trying to pull us off alone mentally and physically to destroy us. When we are aware of the path and make a decision to go off the path through physical, mental attack afterwards the emotional flow happens. If we had tasted of the goodness of God we start feeling alone. Feeling alone and realizing that our actions separated us from our covering our righteousness leaves us feeling helpless. This is the plan of the adversary to use that abandonment and helpless feeling will cause us to hide ourselves and destroy ourselves.

So when Adam cried out that "I was flood with an emotional flow and that made me feel abandon helpless and my reaction was to hide," God very first stage was to speak upon a masterful revelation. Understand many have not yet understood that this revelation for victory was hidden at the time but the process of release was measured throughout time.

Now this brings us to the verses, "And unto Adam he said, Because thou hast hearkened unto the voice of thy wife, and hast eaten of the tree, of which I commanded thee, saying, Thou shalt not eat of it: cursed is the ground for thy sake; in sorrow shalt thou eat of it all the days of thy life; Thorns also and thistles shall it bring forth to thee; and thou shalt eat herb of the field; In the sweat of thy face shalt thou eat bread, till thou return unto the ground; for out of it wast thou taken; for dust thou art, and unto dust shalt thou return. And Adam called his wife's name Eve; because she was the mother of all living. Unto Adam also and to his wife did the LORD God make coats of skins, and clothed them." (Genesis 3:17-21)

Those verses release the great magnitude of the spoken words of our Lord. It let us know that spiritually when sin has strip us of our righteousness that it is the blood that will cover us. This was the introduction to the next stage of the awesome plan of God.

Each and every stage of understanding lead us deeper and deeper into the understanding of God's word. So in the beginning it was just read then it was understood then it was explored and now the revelation is crying out to be heard. Remember that the earth is crying out for the sons of God to be manifested and this will only happen through the revelation of God's word.

So what did God say that marked the start of the world's greatest plan ever? The word records, "and I will put enmity between thee and the woman, and between thy seed and her seed; it shall bruise thy head, and thou shalt bruise his heel." (Genesis 3:15) This is important because when we are equip with the truth then the truth shall break all bondage against us. The truth will set us free from the adversary taking us off our path. So understanding what Adam reveal gives us the eyes to see and understand the attack plan of the adversary. Now that we know how he attacks then we need to know how to withstand the attack. The only way to do that is to know the truth about God greatest gift.

So God spoke it out in Genesis 3:15 then He release it in covenant form in Abraham. Now I will not cover everything but I will hit on some points to show some understanding. (To cover everything it would be another book just wait it will be coming soon.) The Bible records, "And he said unto him, Take me an heifer of three years old, and a she goat of three years old, and a ram of three years old, and a turtledove, and a young pigeon. And he took unto him all these and divided them in the midst, and laid each piece one against another but the birds divided he not. And when the fowls came down upon the carcasses, Abram drove them away. And when the sun was going down, a deep sleep fell upon Abram; and lo, an horror of great darkness fell upon him.

And he said unto Abram, Know of a surety that thy seed shall be a stranger in a land that is not theirs, and shall serve them; and they shall afflict them four hundred years; And also that nation whom they shall serve will I judge: and afterward shall they come out with great substance. And thou shalt go to thy fathers in peace, thou shalt be buried in a good old age. But in the fourth generation they shall come hither again: for the iniquity of the Amorites is not yet full. And it came to pass, that, when the sun went down, and it was dark, behold a smoking furnace, and a burning lamp that passed between those pieces. In the same day the LORD made a covenant with Abram, saying, Unto thy seed have I given this land from the river of Egypt unto the great river, the river Euphrates;." (Genesis 15: 9-18)

Now that is known as the Abrahamic Covenant and we are going to look at just a part of it as well as define it in order to receive from it. In order to understand what I am about to say we first must understand the steps in a covenant in biblical demonstration. In ancient times the blood covenant was common among almost all the people of the Middle East. It was a way of establishing a binding contract between two men. What we call the Old and New Testaments could easily be called the Old and New Covenants. The typical blood covenant contained nine parts, or steps. Here are the steps,

1. The two people exchange coats or robes. (To a Hebrew, the coat or robe represented the person himself, so when he offered the other person his

robe, he was offering himself even unto death.)
2. They take off their belt and offer it to the other person. The belt also called the girdle, was used to hold your sward, your knife and other fighting instruments. (In this way you were saying to the other person that you were offering him your protection. If someone attacks you, they also have them to deal with.)
3. Cut the covenant, in this part an animal or animals is killed and cut down the middle and the two halves are laid opposite each other. The two parties to the covenant pass between the two halves of the animal or animals. (This is saying, May God do so to me and more if I break this covenant. This is a blood covenant and cannot be broken.)
4. Raise the right arm and cut the palm of the hand and clasp each others

hand and mingle their blood. (This is saying to the other person, we are becoming one with each other. TO intermingle the blood is to intermingle the very life of both people.)

5. Exchange names, each one takes part of the others name and incorporates it into their own.
6. Make a scar or some identifying mark. The scar was the outward evidence of the covenant that others could see and know that the covenant was made. Sometimes they would rub the cut in the hand to make a scar, then anyone who wanted to fight you would know that he not only had to fight you but another as well.
7. Give terms of the covenant. Both parties to the covenant stand before a witness and list all of their assets and liabilities, because each one takes all of these upon himself. (You

are saying everything I have is yours and everything you have belong to him. If something happen to then your covenant partner will see to your wife and children.

8. Eat the memorial meal. A loaf of bread is broken in half. Each feeds his half to the other saying, "This is my body, and I am now giving it to you." Then take the wine as a symbol of his blood and says, "This is my blood which is now your blood."

9. Plant a memorial tree. The two them plant a tree as a memorial to the covenant and sprinkle it with the blood of the animal that was killed for the covenant offering.

These nine steps do not have to take place in the same order that they are listed here. There are a lot of covenants listed in the Bible and there is not great detail about them because everyone is familiar with the procedure and the writer understood that. Now we are going to zero in on a particular part of those scriptures to bring out the awesomeness of the revealing of God's word. We don't have time to go through the entire covenant but I truly believe that there are so revealing going on in our spirits now because the Holy Spirit is confirming some things in us.

The old covenant was made with Abram and we have a record of it in the Bible. We can look in on it starting in the fifteenth chapter of Genesis. The Bible says, "After these things the word of the Lord came to Abram in a vision, saying, Do not fear, Abram, I am thy shield, and thy exceeding great reward." (Genesis 15:1) Here we see God offering His robe and belt to Abram, He offers to be his shield and His rewards. He cuts the covenant a few verses later, "And he said unto him, I am the LORD that brought thee out of Ur of the Chaldees, to give thee this land to inherit it. And he said, Lord God, whereby shall I know that I shall inherit it? And he said unto him, Take me an heifer of three years old, and a she goat of three years old, and a ram of three years old, and a turtledove, and a young pigeon. And he took unto him all these and divided them in the midst, and laid each piece one against another but the birds divided he not. And when the fowls came down upon the carcasses, Abram drove them away. And when the sun was going down, a deep sleep fell upon Abram; and lo, an horror of great darkness fell upon him.

And he said unto Abram, Know of a surety that thy seed shall be a stranger in a land that is not theirs, and shall serve them; and they shall afflict them four hundred years; And also that nation whom they shall serve will I judge: and afterward shall they come out with great substance. And thou shalt go to thy fathers in peace, thou shalt be buried in a good old age. But in the fourth generation they shall come hither again: for the iniquity of the Amorites is not yet full. And it came to pass, that, when the sun went down, and it was dark, behold a smoking furnace, and a burning lamp that passed between those pieces. In the same day the LORD made a covenant with Abram, saying, Unto thy seed have I given this land from the river of Egypt unto the great river, the river Euphrates; The Kenites, and the Kenizzites, and the Kadmonites, And the Hittites, and the Perizzites, and the Rephaims, And the Amorites, and the Canaanites, and the Girgashites and the Jebusites. (Genesis 15:7-21)

Here God is giving the terms of the covenant to Abram. But who are the ones passing between the pieces while Abram is in the deep sleep? Now this is the area that I want to focus on so we can see how the release worked. The Bible says, "And it came to pass, that when the sun went down, and it was dark, behold a smoking furnace, and a burning lamp that passed between those pieces." (Genesis 15:17) Now remember "Cut the Covenant" is where the animals are gathered and cut in half and laid opposite of each other and the two that making the covenant pass between them. As they pass through them they are saying, "May God do so to me and more if I break this covenant." This is a blood covenant and cannot be broken.

Now empowered with that information it seems as if there is a mystery or a hidden message here. If the smoking furnace represent God, Himself then it is released that God is making the covenant with Abram through the burning lamp, Jesus Christ. The Bible says, "His head and his hairs were white like wool, as white as snow; and his eyes were as a flame of fire. And his feet like unto fine brass, as if they burned in a furnace; and his voice as the sound of many waters. (Revelation 1:14-15) We see Christ standing in for Abram as a descendant of Abram because God knew that Abram could not keep it. The reason is that God was making a covenant that was a blood covenant that could not be broken and in that it had to be kept perfectly or there was consequences.

In Genesis 17:4, 5, 15 the Bible says, "As for me, behold, my covenant is with thee, and thou shalt be a father of many nations. Neither shall thy name any more be called Abraham; for a father of many nations have I made thee. And God said unto Abraham, As for Sarai thy wife, thou shalt not call her name Sarai, but Sarah shall her name be." In Hebrew, God was called YHWH. Here we see Him taking part of His name combining it with that of Abram and Sarai. Form that time on God was known as "The God of Abraham."

Then we move to the scar or symbol of the covenant. The Bible says, "This is my covenant, which ye shall keep between me and you and thy seed after thee; Every man child among you shall be circumcised. And ye shall circumcise the flesh of your foreskin; and it shall be a token of the covenant betwixt me and you. And he that is eight days old shall be circumcised among you, every man child in your generations, he that is born in the house, or bought with money of any stranger, which is not of thy seed." (Genesis 17:10-12)

The scar of circumcision bears witness of the covenant. Abraham was tested when God told him to sacrifice his only son Isaac on a small mountain called mount Mariah near the town of Salem. Abraham passed the test. Two thousand years ago, the other party to the covenant was to sacrifice His only Son. The names had been change by then; Salem was then called Jerusalem, and Mariah had been changed to Calvary, but the places were the same.

Now we see the miraculous plan being released in the Covenant with Abraham. Then our awesome God took us to the next level as He revealed the makeup and concept within the Ark of the Covenant. In understanding that the

Shittim Wood signify "On the Lord merits" and the understanding how God speak it then released it unto us we have a deeper foundation within Christ. From the very beginning God's plan was awesome and He wanted us to be able to stand against the adversary. If we combine all of the information for me and you this means that it is never by us it is always by him. Our foundation should be built on Him and our movements should be led by Him.

By understanding the attack process by our adversary we see the depths in securing our understanding spiritual keys that unlocks our source to us. In realizing that we are God's creation that is able to obtain and do great things from a simple place because it not us. This all falls upon us because it is whom we belong and what we are attached to. If we belong to God and is attached to His ministry then the things that we are doing will be beyond us as others see us. If we hold fast to the fact that because we come from places that don't seem much and our lives have been tossing and turning that our Lord still can use us.

Our Lord can take the common and do the uncommon with it. He can take the worried the ill and turn it into a stable testimony that set others on fire. He can confused the learned with those of know education. Our Lord is look for those that foundation is not built on them but anchored in Him. Our Lord is looking for those that is willing for Him to build not those that are trying to tell Him what to build. Praise God for the Shittim Wood, on His merit and His righteousness.

Chapter Two

Gold

Now we are traveling in an area that have a lot of mystery but is rewarding when we can understand exactly what is said. The Bible says, "And they shall make an ark of shittim wood: two cubits and a half shall be the length thereof, and a cubit and a half the breadth thereof, and a cubit and a half the height thereof. And thou shalt overlay it with pure gold, within and without shalt thou overlay it, and shalt make upon it a crown of gold round about. And thou shalt cast four rings of gold for it, and put them in the four corners thereof; and two rings shall be in the one side of it, and two rings in the other side of it. And thou shalt make staves of shittim wood, and overlay them with gold. And thou shalt put the staves into the rings by the sides of the ark that the ark may be borne with them.

The staves shall be in the rings of the ark; they shall not be taken from it. And thou shalt make put into the ark the testimony which I shall give thee. And thou shalt make a mercy seat of pure gold: two cubits and a half shall be the length thereof, and a cubit and half the breadth thereof. And thou shalt make two cherubims of gold, of beaten work shalt thou make them, in the two ends of the mercy seat. And make one cherub on the one end, and the other cherub on the other end: even of the mercy seat shall ye make the cherubims on the two ends thereof." (Exodus 25:10-19)

We are going to focus in on the "Gold" that seems to have great importance to our Lord. Now we are not going to reveal nothing that has not been told but what we are going to do is to bring all the things together so we can see the fullness of the word. First the foundation is built on nothing but the "merits of God and His righteousness." So one the Shittim Wood was gather then God said overlay it with pure gold. Now it is very interesting that "pure gold" was used. But before we get into this we have to realize that there is many theories on how gold is formed. The different theories itself are very interesting to me because it is fascinating how man tries to intellectualize the power of God.

Exactly how is gold formed? No one knows for sure. The story around this rare metal is truly an enigma. No one knows how it was formed and who first discovered it. For thousands of years, gold has been one of the world's most precious commodities. Valued by every major civilization of record, gold still remains as powerful now as it did in ancient times, perhaps because of the mystery involving its origins. The following hypotheses suggest how gold came to be:

The Greek Theory: Gold was probably first spotted in a stream, and Greek philosophers believed gold was a combination of water and sunlight.

The Hot Water Theory: Surprisingly, the most popular of the three hypothesis is a complex variation on the primitive idea that gold is a combination of water and sunlight. This hypothesis states that circulating pools of ground water were heated by volcanoes and molten rock, and then pushed into crevices in the earth's surface. The water went several miles into the earth's surface. As the heated water contacted the mineral-rich crust, it began dissolving the metals in the bedrocks. When the water eventually reached a cooler surface, a unique, gold-like metal formed.

The Magma Theory: The second hypothesis presupposes that the elements that create gold are present and expelled from volcanic magma as it cools. Because granite rocks are solidified magma, this hypothesis especially holds true for gold found near or inside this type of rock.

The Hot Rock Theory: The third hypothesis concerns gold found in volcanic rocks. It states the rocks were heated at high temperatures and pressurized, which created a chemical reaction. As the temperatures cooled and pressure decreased, the rock expelled mineral-rich water. The minerals in this water eventually created gold.

The presence of gold in both water and earth helps explain the various techniques for gathering this precious metal. For example, prospectors panned for gold in California during the Gold Rush, and companies and individual miners have been exploring promising gold deposits for years. So this metal has been a very powerful thing in searching for it and obtaining it.

These different theories have very interesting outcomes in regards to the forming of gold. Now this is interesting because some try to elude from the presence of God in the forming of the gold, but we don't know how God actually do it. But what is remarkable is that this particular metal has many different applications and hold a significant meaning not only to mankind but to God as well. Regardless how it is developed we are going to take a look at why this particular metal is so important to God. Now once gold is found and dug out of the earth then there is a process of smelting and other things.

A smelter does more than just melt the gold into a bar. Gold smelting is the process by which impurities are removed from the gold. This is accomplished by using pressure, heat, and certain chemicals. Once the process is complete, the smelter is left with a remarkably pure material.

The first step of the smelting process involves processing the raw ore. The gold material is pulverized into fine particles. These particles are then placed into a furnace that has reached a temperature above gold's melting point. This burns off many of the impurities found in gold but not all.

The second step involves the introduction of chemicals to separate the pure gold from other minerals and metals. The chemicals that are typically used are potassium cyanide and mercury. These two chemicals cause the melted gold to coagulate and form pure nuggets.

Once the gold ore and scrap gold have been refined, the gold is placed back into the furnace to be melted one more time. This pure gold is melted then poured into a mold to form ingots. Ingots are essentially gold bars and come in a variety of shapes and sizes. This pure gold can be used to make a variety of electrical components, jewelry or it can simply be used as a store of value.

Gold smelting is not a complicated process, but it does require specialized equipment. Would be gold investors should be aware of the process before they purchase raw ore. Raw ore is cheaper than pure, smelted gold because it contains impurities. When purchasing gold ore, investors are also purchasing the worthless material that clings to gold. If purchasing gold as an investment, it is a better option to purchase already smelted gold.

Now the Bible says, "And they shall make an ark of shittim wood: two cubits and a half shall be the length thereof, and a cubit and a half the breadth thereof, and a cubit and a half the height thereof. And thou shalt overlay it with pure gold, within and without shalt thou overlay it, and shalt make upon it a crown of gold round about. And thou shalt cast four rings of gold for it, and put them in the four corners thereof; and two rings shall be in the one side of it, and two rings in the other side of it. And thou shalt make staves of shittim wood, and overlay them with gold. And thou shalt put the staves into the rings by the sides of the ark that the ark may be borne with them.

The staves shall be in the rings of the ark; they shall not be taken from it. And thou shalt make put into the ark the testimony which I shall give thee. And thou shalt make a mercy seat of pure gold: two cubits and a half shall be the length thereof, and a cubit and half the breadth thereof. And thou shalt make two cherubims of gold, of beaten work shalt thou make them, in the two ends of the mercy seat. And make one cherub on the one end, and the other cherub on the other end: even of the mercy seat shall ye make the cherubims on the two ends thereof." (Exodus 25:10-19)

Now what is so powerful about this is the fact that God said "pure gold" and this was very specific. We as members of the Body of Christ have to see that when the process is started it is not the form that is used. This should explode in our spirits because it shows not only a spiritual form of us but it shows the great love that God has for us. Many times we view ourselves and judge ourselves to the point that we even want to be someone else or we call ourselves names. This is a deception of the adversary by way of a delusion because of the lack of knowledge. We gain strength from our past experiences and the knowledge that we receive that we can build on. If we stand on the purity of the word of God then we can face anything.

Let us look at this regardless of how it is formed we want to look at the product that is brought out. We see that this raw ore, it does not mean that it is not gold but it not the gold by itself. This is interesting because we see that with the gold there is other materials that lessen the value of the product but the product the gold value has not change. So this reflect on us so strongly because from birth through our journey we see that we are wrapped in no good thing but once we receive Him then we become a vessel for God to use. In that we have to understand that from the beginning we are wrapped with something else but the true product is still there.

Now when the raw material is gathered it has to be then pulverized into fine particles. Pulverized to crush, pound or grind into powder. The very first step is to completely destroy or break down the raw material which is done by force. In order to do this there is great pressure place upon the raw ore. Now physically in the natural realm we can comprehend this because we have hit things with hammers or other objects and saw the shattering effect. For some of us we get a great kick out of crushing things just to see it splatter into a hundred pieces. But how do this come over into the spiritual. We have to come to an understanding that God could use anything to cover the shittim wood. But He was very pacific in choosing every part of the materials used in the building of the Ark of the Covenant.

In order to grasps the great magnitude of this into the spiritual realm for us we have to follow a magnificent truths. First and foremost that we don't search for God we react to the calling of our Lord. The misconception is that we go looking for God but God makes the first step. The

Bible says, "Jesus answered them, I told you and ye believed not: the works that I do in my Father's name, they bear witness of me. But ye believe not, because ye are not of my sheep; as I said unto you. My sheep hear my voice, and I know them, and they follow me: And I give unto them eternal life; and they shall never perish, neither shall any man pluck them out of my hand. My Father, which gave them me, is greater than all; and no man is able to pluck them out of my Father's hand. I am my Father are one." (John 10:25-30)

God makes the first move reaching toward us and once we are in the fold there is nothing that can take us out. Now for many of us as the Lord reach toward us we are in certain positions of life. Some of us have so much on us till we are about to lose our minds. For others there is a situation or circumstance that causes us to seek out every avenue until there is nothing else but God. For others it is simply a longing of emptiness a space that we cannot fill and we try some of everything to fill it. In any case we have to see that most of us exhaust every avenue before we turn to God. In that sense we can see the magnificent of the revelation of the gold process. Let us take a look at this a see what is there.

The very first thing is to put the gold ore under tremendous pressure to crush it into fine dust. For some we are beaten mentally for others it is physical but the end results are the same. We are brought down to a position that is weak exhausted. For some we are at the lowest point in our lives. For others it is the scariest time in our lives and others it is the most loneliness time that we have ever experience. All of our own resources have failed and all those that we have depended on have failed and it seems that we have been dropped in a pit and cannot get out. We have been beaten crush into a lump that is just existing and not living we are the walking dead.

These types of feelings beats up from the inside out. Our emotions are drain and our spirits are weak our hearts are heavy. This eventually will start taking it toil upon us and in our physical realm it is seen upon us. Some of us are sent to doctors because we cannot express what is going on with us but we just feel out of it. We are given medication and go to different counseling but nothing changes. We turn to friends alcohol drugs each other for pleasure and nothing feels the void of hurt loneliness, guilt, sorrow, and every other anchor that the adversary can use to attempt to destroy us. But for most in order for us to reach up we have to be beaten down crush abandon then from the depths of our souls we cry out.

So from the beginning of the process we are identified and our Lord was making a statement with the process. Physically the children of Israel could see the gold handlers dig out the ore. Where some of us feel that we are just overwhelmed buried in every negative feeling that exist. Our Lord reaches from up high down low in the pit to touch us that causes us to look up. As they watched the gold handlers' pound on this ore and beat this ore we see the spiritual representation of us being weaken to a point to where we can be used by our Lord. We are now in the position that as on actor put "There is no other place but up."

Now we going to drop a nugget upon you, when the pressure is applied to the gold ore by way of grinding or pounding the weight of the piece change as it is transformed from solid to powder. Some stuff that is attached to the gold ore fly away other stuff density changes and what was a hundred pound is now eight to sixty pounds now. It is the transformation through the grinding and pounding that some stuff is lifted of it. Now for us when we are in those positions and circumstances that have beaten us down and have strip us of all of our resources and we reach up and the Lord latch on to us He pulls us out of the pit. As He pulls us out of the pit there are something that just are left behind. There are something that falls off as well and we feel the burdens lifted off our shoulders. As the bounding of the weight of sorrow embarrassment, confusion, pain lay upon us and we cry out and reach up God's Spirit blows it away.

Each of us have our own experiences and our own journey but our connection is through the pit and the power of the resurrected Savior. This is powerful because for many of us there was one question that many of us cried out we have said, "Why Me?" In that I want you to know that the reason it was you is because it was Him that have reached out to you because He loves you. Understand that God saw us before we saw our reflection in the mirror and wanted nothing but the best for us. At the time of the grinding it don't seem like it but God knows if we continue on the path that we are own that the destruction will be much worse. God knows that our destiny in Him will be greater than anything we can possibly imagine. When we are crying out "Why Me" God is crying out "Why Not Me!"

Sometimes in order to get a child to understand that there safety place is here we have to give them something that impact them that causes them to come over here. For some to get them to come over is a nudge for others is a stern voice or look for some we have to have a backside touch. But regardless of what is needed our Father know exactly what we need in order to be within the safety of His loving arms and empowered by His Spirit. So when we see another going through the process of the pounding and being beaten down to a position that God is calling them to look up and reach up fall to your knees and begin to pray for wholeness. Many of us tries to fix things that God is trying to destroy in order to save. The process is a calling and we have to answer in order to hear the Master say welcome home my child.

Now phase two in the process is the mixing. The second step involves the introduction of chemicals to separate the pure gold from other minerals and metals. The chemicals that are typically used are potassium cyanide and mercury. Now this is very important because it is the break down section by way of mixing certain chemicals into the fine powder to cause more of the natural material to come forth. This particular step will help in releasing more of the impurities to achieve a level of material that can be elevated to the next level. This takes away the material that has latched on so hard that it takes something else to remove it.

Now in the spiritual realm this is very revealing because of the use of this particular steps connects directly to us. If we take a good look at this step within our spiritual lives we would leap for joy. Let us take a look when we call upon the Lord within the position that we are in God is faithful and He will show up. When He shows up forgiveness comes within sanctification comes with Him healing comes with Him and victory comes with Him. Now that is a punch that empowers us to stand up or get up to be released from whatever has us bond. In that we feel an instant relief because weight has been lifted up off of us and now we begin the process of total victory. For some we begin to receive exactly what we need at the moment to overcome. For others we are given exactly what we need to go through. Regardless it is a victory for the glory of God.

Then the Lord, Himself brings in other parts of Him that function is to strip us of all impurities. In other words God has dug up the raw us or the raw ore out of being pounded and now He begins a process that strips us. Many are confused about this process because of so much teaching that point fingers and proceed to introduce things that has nothing to do with God but man's religion. The Bible says, "If ye love me, keep my commandments. And I will pray the Father, and he shall give you another Comforter, that he may abide with you forever. Even the Spirit of truth; whom the world cannot receive because it seeth him not, neither knoweth him: but ye know him, for he dwelleth with you, and shall be in you. I will not leave you comfortless I will come to you." (John 14:15-18)

For us this a powerful release by Jesus as He stated these recorded words because it is a part of God that has been given. Jesus was aware of the past representation of the Comforter or Holy Spirit and was gathering the past understanding and presenting a future revelation. Many times because of what we called diluting the word the adversary has crept in and presenting a delusion. Many want to twist the word or make it fit their belief instead of looking and receiving the truth of the word.

We understand first, "Ye have not chosen me, but I have chosen you, and ordained you, that ye should go and bring forth fruit, and that your fruit should remain that whatsoever ye shall ask of the Father in my name, he may give it you." (John 15:16) God chose us. In that revealing once we step into the choosing of the Lord or the calling then the word says, "If ye keep my commandments ye shall abide in my love; even as I have kept my Father's commandments and in his love. These things have I spoken unto you, that my joy might remain in you, and that your joy might be full. This is my commandment, That ye love one another, as I have loved you. Greater love hath no man that this that a man lay down his life for his friends. Ye are my friends if ye do whatsoever I command you. Henceforth I call you not servants for the servant knoweth not what his lord doeth; but I have called you friends; for all things that I have heard of my Father I have made known unto you." (John 15:10-15)

What some missed is that when we come into the kingdom of God that there is a placement that is very important for us? We see in those scriptures that we are in Christ and Christ is in His Father and that merging is capable because of love and obedience. Now many take this and run with it but if we look with clear eyes instead preconceive assumptions we would not have any problem here. Jesus understood what was being ushered in at this time but He wanted us to know that what was coming did not disregard the old it enhance it so you and I would be spotless. Jesus knew that merging was because of love and obedience and for you and I that is not in us from the beginning.

We were in the position of beaten down and have no idea how to live this life on this side. But at the moment of conversion some have no clue of the word of God and others just have no comprehension of it yet we just know we need Jesus. That is the covering for us is Jesus and in Him is the grace that was issued out and places us into our position. Grace is forgiveness and that forgiveness locks us into position in Christ and Christ in the Father. Now what we need to change our thinking or renew our minds is with us and everything we need to know is given unto us. We have His word and His might to overcome those things that are not of God by way of God.

Then the word says, "But when the Comforter is come, whom I will send unto you from the Father, even the Spirit of truth, which proceedeth from the Father, he shall testify of me; And ye also shall bear witness because ye have been with me from the beginning." (John 15:26-27) Now we have heard many say that, "I don't know what the

Lord want me to do?" Here Christ had brought together the beginning the present and the future within these two powerful verses. Now remember that He said, " He chosen us" now in that we know that He had to know us and then He said, "been with him from the beginning". Now we have to know that not only do the words of our Lord go through the physical it also regenerate in the spiritual realm as well. So in Christ was reminding you and I that from the beginning He knew us and we had been called and from that place as we step into our call then He will be released to us through the Comforter. Now as He is released unto us by way of our renewing of our mind then He He will give us something to do testify of Him.

Now for us we are supposed to fine our way to testify of Him outside of our presence or our daily walk. In other words we are to intentionally let our presence be a representation of our Lord as well as fine a platform to testify from. We can do it through our cooking, our visiting the sick and shut in, we can just mentor whatever but our platform is geared to us to testify of Jesus. This is the greatest and only thing God wants from His people is to just simply tell about Him! But in order to do that or even understand how to do that God release something called a Comforter or Holy Spirit to guide us in that direction. So when we enter into the Body of Christ that we were called to from the beginning we also receive the Comforter.

Here is a nugget, many might say that I am not a speaker or I cannot just talk to people like that, but the Bible says, "Also I say unto you, Whosoever shall confess me before men him shall the Son of man also confess before the angels of God; But he that denieth me before me shall be denied before the angels of God. And whosoever shall speak a word against the Son of man it shall be forgiven him; but unto him that blasphemeth against the Holy Ghost it shall not be forgiven. And when they bring you unto the synagogues and unto magistrates and powers take ye no thought how or what thing ye shall answer, or what ye shall say; For the Holy Ghost shall teach you in the same hour what ye ought to say. (Luke 12:8-12) So if we believe the Word then we have to understand that God knows our weaknesses fears and shortcomings. In that the mix of the Holy Spirit will empower us not through our own power but through Jesus power.

This why the covering of the Shittim wood is performed from the inside out. If we grasp this reality then spiritually we see the revelation. When we come to the knowledge of Jesus we receive a new spirit our old man is replaced with the new man. With that understanding that our inward man is replaced first that causes an eruption from the renewing of the mind the transformation of our outer comes fourth. The transformation comes when we start understanding the grace of God and become obedient to the love of God. We begin to love Him so much because we start truly understanding what it took to bring us to this point. So out of love for Him we start loving ourselves and realizing that there is somethings that we are doing is hindering our growth in Him. We realize some places we go don't have Him in there conversation or action. We realize that there is a voice within us that we are sensitive to that tells us this or that we are doing is not what our Lord wants us to do.

So we are in the process of changing the places we go and the things we do and even say. But remember God wanted pure gold and this involves another process after the mixing of chemicals and this is smelting. Now smelting is taking the gold and placing it into the furnace with high temperature that continues to burn away that which is not gold. Many have this particular process in the spiritual realm confusing to many. Some teach that if a person truly have an experience with Jesus that there is an instant change in their behavior, talk, everything. Some teaches that if we really had an experience an encounter with Jesus then we instantly don't sin any more. Now if we do sin again then our experience was not genuine.

We want you to know as gold goes through the fire we will as well. We are placed into the fire to reveal things about us that is not obvious as well as strengthening. Each of us have a journey that we must go through. In our journey we are being transformed from glory to glory. In order to strip away our impurities some we can drop by way of knowledge. Some of our impurities we will need to release to God and grow in grace to get rid of. We also have some impurities that we know nothing about until it is reveal unto us. We have to understand that the more we grow in grace and the knowledge of Jesus Christ the more we become aware and sensitive to the Holy Spirit. In becoming open layers of the depth of sin is reveal that is wrapped in thinking intentions, motives as well as our actions. So as we open up and get more honest with ourselves and as we are placed in different situations with different degrees of intensity we become aware of our shortcomings, weakness, and lacks.

By being in these intense situations and circumstances as we grow in Christ we begin to recognize the movement of God our faith is increased and our testimony becomes more effective. With this understanding we have to grasp the fact that the natrual pure gold is the spiritual purity of the transformation of the heart that spills outwardly and is seen in the physical transformation of our actions, speaking, wisdom and thinking. This concept is the hidden nugget that transform a weak individual into a mighty force for the kingdom of God. If we see that our trials and tribulations our intense situations and circumstances are not for destruction but for stripping and strengthening then we would have joy in the midst of. You see how we go through is just as important that we go through. If we don't get the lesson out of the intense situations or trials then we will miss the stripping that will empower us. If we miss the strengthening in the situation then we get weaker in our faith. We have to receive that everything is working for our good because our trials strip away that which block our growth and strengthens us to move not by sight.

Spiritual smelting is necessary for growth and moving into the next level in Christ Jesus. Our journeys are designed to bring us into the fullness of Christ that will propell us into our destiny that will be represented in our fruit and works. If we hold fast to God's plan then our destiny will be proven by those that chose the light over darkness because of what they saw in us. This is our highest praise that our life represent Christ to a point that another sees us in the midst and cry out "What must I do to be saved!" So in that God get the glory and all the praise and that is exactly how one here those words at the point of transition "Welcome home my good and faithful servant." Our transformation is our personal journey with its twist and turns that our Lord straightens the path right into His loving arms. Trials tribulations intense situations and circumstances is our stepping stones to God's ordain place for us to be transformed.

Mercy Seat

Now this particular section will be an eye opening truth that will be enlightening and chain breaking revelation. We are entering into a place of revealing and strengthening that will empower God's people to be what they have been ordained to be. Also this section will unlock some mysteries that will unlock the hidden strength that is lock up in us. There have been much confusion about the Mercy Seat and it functions. For most of us we have discarded it for the simple fact that it has nothing to do with us. There are some beliefs that will be challenged and questioned. This particular section is not design to change any minds but to call into clarity of a particular portion of God's word that for some have been evasive. If we pray and seek God empowered with clarity an understanding situations and circumstances will change because of vision and the pointed destiny.

For this section it will be a magnifying look at some scriptures that some believe that the writer pulled out the air. Each of us are at different stages in our journey but we all have to come together in agreement that the most important thing that we get is understanding. Understanding of God's word gives us the ability to apply God's word in our lives. It is a powerful tool or weapon in the hands of a person that understand what the tool or weapon can do. When we grasp the understanding then we also know when the tool is needed as well as the limitation of the weapon or tool. Now many have never heard the word limitation associated with God's word. In order to receive this stay within this journey and continue through with this section and watch an awesome God transform a powerful weapon for the building of the kingdom of God.

The Mercy Seat in Hebrew is Kapporet "atonement piece" the Greek hilasterion is a lid or cover of solid gold of the Ark of the Covenant and it was connected to the Day of Atonement. It also appears twice in the New Testament and we want to start connecting the Old and the New Testament. In order to get the fullness we will have to travel backward and move forward to today. We will have to have a little history to connect us to the present.

In a manner of speaking, the mercy seat concealed the people of God from the ever-condemning judgment of the Law. Each year on the Day of Atonement, the high priest entered the Holy of Holies and sprinkled the blood of animals sacrificed for the atonement of the sins of God's people. This blood was sprinkled on the mercy seat. The point conveyed by this imagery is that it is only through the offering of blood that the condemnation of the Law could be taken away and violations of God's laws covered.

The Greek word for "mercy seat" in Hebrews 9:5 is hilasterion, which means "that which makes expiation" or "propitiation." It carries the idea of the removal of sin. In Ezekiel 43:13-15, the brazen altar of sacrifice is also called hilasterion (the propitiatory or mercy seat) in the Septuagint (the Greek translation of the Old Testament) because of its association with the shedding of blood for sin.

What is the significance of this? In the New Testament, Christ Himself is designated as our "propitiation." Paul explains this in his letter to the Romans: "Being justified freely by His grace through the redemption that is in Christ Jesus, whom God set forth as a propitiation by His blood, through faith, to demonstrate His righteousness, because in His forbearance God had passed over the sins that were previously committed" (Romans 3:24-25 NKJV). What Paul is teaching here is that Jesus is the covering for sin, as shown by these Old Testament prophetic images. By means of His death, and our response to Christ through our faith in Him, all our sins are covered. Also, whenever believers sin, we may turn to Christ who continues to be the propitiation or covering for our sins (1 John 2:1, 4:10). This ties together the Old and New Testament concepts regarding the covering of sin as exemplified by the mercy-seat of God.

We still missed even a greater revealing here because as believers we have the covering of the blood upon us through Christ Jesus. Understand that as a believer we believe on Christ and Christ covers us with His blood and when the Father sees us He sees Christ because of the payment of our sins. In that sense then the led that covers us is the actual sprinkling of the blood of Christ upon the transforming precious Spirit that has been changed.

So what do this mean for us today in our journey and in our day to day living? Many fight over different understanding of backsliding or one being able to do a certain thing and call themselves members of the sect. Paul recorded that, "I find then a law, that, when I would do good, evil is present with me. For I delight in the law of God after the inward man: but I see another law in my members, warring against the law of my mind, and bringing me into captivity to the law of sin which is in my members. O wretched man that I am! who shall deliver me from the body of this death? I thank God through Jesus Christ our Lord. So then with the mind I myself serve the law of God with the flesh the law of sin. (Romans 7:21-25)

This passage of scriptures releases the hidden secrets within the revelation of the secrets for which the Apostle Paul understood from the Mercy Seat from the tabernacle and what Christ did and how it applied to him today and the separation of the truth for which the adversary was trying to do. The Apostle Paul says he finds a law and this is the introduction of the revelation the is the key to unlock the mystery.

The role of law is to administrate the covenant. Laws prohibit things destructive to a relationship with God (e.g., worshiping other gods). The law gives direction to what a loving response to God should be, and tells how to reap the full benefits of the relationship. Viewed from one perspective, the promises formalized by covenant were unconditional; but from an individual's perspective, benefits could be forfeited by disobedience. Disobedience does not automatically invalidate a covenant, any more than a husband's rudeness to a wife he vowed to cherish invalidates his marriage covenant. Yet disobedience mars the relationship, and may reduce its benefits. In the desert a whole generation of Israelites forfeited their covenant benefits (the promised land) through disobedience, yet the covenant continued.

So with this frame of thought the Apostle Paul with not down playing the law but recognizing the breaking of the law with the understanding that it interrupt the relationship between him and Christ. So when he spoke that he recognize that he find a law the Apostle Paul was actual saying that he see the thing within himself that can separate the relationship that he have with Christ that was establish at the beginning of time. In that the Apostle Paul knew the atonement for the separation as well once he recognize exactly what it was.

The Apostle Paul explain, "I would do good but evil is present with me." Now the Apostle recognize that it was something that was hindering him that was right there with him. If we look at the words we see that apparently the evil has to something that the Apostle can not escape from because his words is "I would do good". He wants to do good this is his desire but his desire is not strong enough because the desire is weaker than the evil.

See here is the hidden underline back drop that the Apostle Paul at this time is preaching and teaching the gospel of Jesus Christ. The Apostle Paul at this time in his life is not practicing sin or wrong doing and and doing everything that he can to spread the gospel. What the Apostle is relaying is the struggle within to do what he is doing from a point of how he is able to do it. In other word the Apostle Paul is saying that each day that he wake he recognize that there is a law something that been around from the beginning that is trying to separate my relationship between me and Christ. Each day I try to do good but evil is present with me regardless of what I am doing.

Then the Apostle Paul get descriptive in the exact nature of how this works. He says, "For I delight in the law of God after the inward man:; but I see another law in my members, warring against the law of my mind and bringing me into captivity to the law of sin which is in my members." The Apostle Paul say that the transform man the new man loves the Lord. He says that the renewed Spirit yearn for the the present of the Lord and wants to be with the Lord and craves the Lord and the works of the Lord.

But the Apostle Paul also recognize that the adversary is constantly trying to activate the atmosphere to ignite his members to react outside the will of God. For the Apostle Paul he felt the pressure to give up he felt the pain of being beaten and hungry and most likely what it felt to be without so the adversary used the same tactics that was used in the beginning on him.

The adversary most likely tried to activate the atmosphere to ignite his emotions through his eyes as he did in the beginning with Eve and later with Christ. Most likely because the Apostle knew what it was to be hungry so he tried him with testing the Lord over sustaining himself as he did in the beginning as he did with Christ and most likely he have done with some of us. Then since the Apostle Paul knew what it was to be without he probably tried him with provisions as he did in the beginning as he did with Christ as he is doing today.

The Apostle Paul is recording that the adversary has come to him through different deception against his mind to try to activate his members by igniting the atmosphere by showing him what he could have if he would do this or that and he would not have to go through this or that if the Apostle would only do this or that. The Apostle Paul is letting us know that on a daily journey when he wakes he recognize a law something that from the beginning that have been revealed to him that is trying to disrupt the relationship between him and Christ.

That when he get up he wants to do good but evil is present. That evil is trying to ignite the atmosphere to cause his member to over take him by way of activating his mind as he struggles to do the will of the inward man. So he is having some trouble so pitfalls that is directly design to make it tough to turn him around. The Apostle Paul is having some against him purposefully to cause him to think about going on.

But the Apostle knew who to turn to in order to get what he needed because he knew this was going on regardless of what he was doing. The Apostle Paul said, "O wretched man that I am! who shall deliver me from the body of this death? I thank God through Jesus Christ our Lord. So then with the mind I myself serve the law of God but with the flesh the law of sin."

The Apostle Paul realized that because of what was established from the beginning as of the fall of mankind and he was born into and the wickedness that is naturally in man's heart, that is truly provoked by the ignition of the atmosphere by the adversary, that he was truly able of living in degradation and misery. The Apostle understood that it was nothing that he was able to do that could stop this or change this or even fight this off because what was with him was stronger, smarter and been around since the beginning. This is what the Apostle Paul meant when he cried out "wretched" to describe his disposition.

For us this is very important to understand because it never about what we perceive about our good works or our good acts trying to weigh the scale out. We can never get caught up in because we never did this or that we are a good person because the intentions of what we did nullify everything. What we tend to forget that one act of sin disqualify us before a Holy God. But the Apostle Paul knew that from the beginning our God had set a plan into motion to counter act a separation that was coming through Jesus Christ and he thank God for it.

See the Apostle Paul understood the whole picture that from the beginning the separation was the plan from the adversary. But the separation had a flaw because it could not be forever because God had reversal power. God knew that we needed His mercy through sacrifice for payment of sin. Now through the forty-two generations through the different elements of introduction God instituted a plan that took a stationary piece a lifted it to His right hand.

Mercy is compassion or forgiveness shown toward someone whom it is within one's power to punish or harm:

and this is an on going thing for us. Remember sin deserve punishment because of what sin does. Sin separate us from the God that proved His love by sending His only Son to pay for sin. In that case when we sin we are asking Christ to pay that price again in a spiritual sense. But the word of God let us know that He only had to be sacrifice once. The Bible says, "By the which will we are sanctified through the offering of the body of Jesus Christ once for all." (Hebrews 10:10)

A perfect sacrifice an unblemished man that knew know sin slain for the righteousness of God as payment of sin. The Bible says, "For the having a shadow of good things to come, and not the very image of the things, can never with those sacrifices which they offered year by year continually make the comers thereunto perfect. For then would they not have ceased to be offered? because that the worshipers once purged should have had no more conscience of sins. But in those sacrifices there is remembrance again made of sins every year. For it is not possible that the blood of bulls and of goats should take away sins." (Hebrews 10:1-4)

The Bible also says, "But Christ being come an high priest of good things to come, by a greater and more perfect tabernacle, not made with hands, that is to say, not of this building; neither by the blood of goats and calves, but by his own blood he entered in once into the holy place, having obtained eternal redemption for us." (Hebrews 9:11-12) So we see the spiritual truth that Christ stepped once into the heavenly realm into the Holy of Holies and sprinkle His blood upon the mercy seat as our High Priest as the slaughtered Lamb of God.

So here is the catch when Christ is accepted into our heart He enter as the King of Kings and Lord of Lord as our Savior. Now what we miss is that He is also the sacrifice the blood that is sprinkled upon the Mercy Seat because we miss the revelation. We are the one that God loves so much that were created in His image and was separated from Him. We are the one that God instituted a plan to restore and bring back unto Him His glory through His only begotten Son.

In order for God to bring us back we had to have a payment for our sin the blood had to cover us and that is exactly what Jesus does. Jesus Christ cover that what deserves to be punished with His blood so the Lord Himself sees redemption instead of rejection. God did not tell Israel to put the blood over the tabernacle and the death angel will pass them by. The Bible says, "And they shall take of the blood, and strike it on the two side posts and on the upper door post of the houses, wherein they shall eat it." (Exodus 12:7) We see that it went on each house and when God saw the blood His death angel would pass them by.

Mercy Seat is the covering and our covering is the blood that cries out unto the Lord forgiveness. Each member of the Body of Christ has been sprinkled with the blood supernaturally and spiritually for a divine connection to the heavenly host the empower us and strengthen us to move through the shadow of the valley of death and death pass us by, Praise God!

Angels And That's Within

Many of us have to understand the alignment of God's order and the power thereof. Many have been flooded with different types of ministries teachings and denominational beliefs and we have been bombarded with information of spiritual self help guru seminars. We seen the different info commercials that we can get this water or this different blanket or handkerchief or this or that but we seemed to be in the same spot wanting. We have so much fleshly desires that are so out of control that the adversary has infiltrated our worship places with this false teaching.

We have to get back to the root of the source of the truth in order to break free of the hold of the demonic influence of the adversary. We as members of the Body of Christ is truly missing the signs and wonders that should follow us as believers because we are diluting God's ministry with our wanting and calling it God's ministry. We are caught up with size, looks, materialism and other things of this world that we are missing revelation, spiritual enhancement, restoration. Let us continue and look at the remaining elements and see if God's truth pops out.

If we see that on top of the Ark of Covenant there are two cherubim that are facing each other. On top of the

Mercy Seat the two cherubim face each other and in between them is where the glory of God would appear. Now most theologians attempt to explain this from the top outward. But for me I want to explain it from the inside out. Now my reason for this is because our Lord works from the inside outward. The Bible says, "For it is God which worketh in you both to will and to do of his good pleasure." (Philippians 2:13)

The Bible says, "Neither pray I for these alone, but for them also which shall believe on me through their word; that they all may be one; as thou, Father, art in me, and I in thee, that they also may be one in us; that the world may believe that thou hast sent me. And the glory which thou gavest me I have given them that they may be one even as we are one. I in them, and thou in me, that they may be made perfect in one; and that the world may know that thou hast sent me, and and hast loved them, as thou hast loved me. Father I will that they also, whom thou hast given, me be with me where I am; that they may behold my glory, which thou hast given me: for thou lovedst me before the foundation of the world." (John 17:20-24)

The Bible also records, "For many are called, but few are chosen." (Matthew 22:14) Also the Bible records, "For God so loved the world, that he gave his only begotten Son, that whosoever believeth in him should not perish, but have eternal life." (John 3:16) Now in looking at these passage of scripture we know that our Lord plan was put into place that His Son died for all. God loved us all enough regardless of when we were going to be born where we were going to be born or how we were going to be born He loved us enough that HE sent His son to die for our sin to build our relationship back to Him.

Now here is the thing it not about free will how we determine it but it all about mercy and grace. Understand it was not our free will that brought Christ death upon mankind. It was not our free will that release Christ from His heavenly place to be took from judgment hall to judgment hall. It was not our free will that placed Him upon the cross and cause men to spit upon Him and mock Him and strike Him. It was love that brought Him and sin that sent Him. This is what it means that all have come short of the glory of of God that our sin placed Him upon the cross regardless of how we want to name it.

So the call is out to all but not everyone is going to believe on the name of Jesus Christ. Some are not going to believe that they need a Savior or in heaven or hell. Now here is the step ladder understanding those that do believe is not that they were picked by God like they were special but our Lord know the beginning as well as He knows the end. God knows our thoughts before we get the thought so our actions He knows before we do it. Now for some this concept is hard to comprehend because if God knows all this then why don't He intervein when certain things happen. If God move in the manner of stopping this or that then the choices we make would make no difference because regardless of the choice God will correct the wrong ones.

In order for us to be individuals we have to be accountable for the choices we make. So if we make certain choices even if God knows that the choice will cost so many lives He have to let the choice stand because we have to be accountable for the choice because we are individuals. If God made our choices then it would not have been no need for Christ to come because Eve never would have beaten from the tree. In that case God never would have let His Son be beaten and spit upon for declared people that hate Him, murders, liars, and all those that stand against Him.

So God know the ones that going to make the true choice those that are given to His Son and there is a few things that will mark there truth. Within the Ark of the Covenant was the rod of Aaron. Now the rod of Aaron signified the choice that God had chosen him by way of budding and producing almonds. So first and for most the rod represented that the call was sent out and the acceptance was there and God had known and chosen because He knew the heart of the individual because He knows the future in this person.

The rod of Aaron also represent the priestly representation regardless because for us the High Priest has taken His position within our hearts. The rod of Aaron also represent the connection that we have between this plain and the spiritual plain as well as the connection the heavenly host. Now for us if we realize that within us spiritually we have the rod of Aaron representation within us and if we move in that then we can walk through some stuff that we been stop by.

Remember that we are the chosen ones we are the ones that budded without any assistance from any other elements but the heavenly host. We have been called out not just to be put through persecution but to come out of persecution to be glorified by God so that He be glorified through us.We have to remember that the rod of Aaron did a miraculous thing so that makes us a miracle. The understanding to a miracle is that if we are a miracle then we always a miracle. A miracle holds power and stands on the strength that performs the miracle. A miracle stays connect to the source of the miracle because it is connect to the miracle make. So the rod of Aaron represent chosen, acceptance, priest, connection, produce and miracle Praise God!

Now the Bible records, "I beseech you therefore, brethren, by the mercies of God, that ye present your bodies a living sacrifice, holy, acceptable unto God, which is your reasonable service. And be not conformed to this world: but be ye transformed by the renewing of your mind, that ye may prove what is that good, and acceptable, and perfect, will of God. (Romans 12:1-2)

The Bible also records, "But continue in the things which thou hast learned and hast been assured of, knowing of whom thou hast learned them; and that from a child thou hast known the holy scriptures, which are able to make thee wise unto salvation through faith which is in Christ Jesus. All scripture is given by inspiration of God, and is profitable for doctrine, for reproof, for correction, for instruction in righteousness: that the man of God may be perfect, throughly furnished unto all good works." (2 Timothy 3:14-17)

The Bible records, "For I say, through the grace given unto me, to every man that is among you, not to think of himself more highly than he ought to think, but to think soberly, according as God hath dealt to every man the measure of faith." (Romans 12:3) One more the Bible records, "Wherefore, as by one man sin entered into the world, and death by sin; and so death passed upon all men, for that all have sinned; (for until the law sin was in the world: but sin is not imputed when there is no law. Nevertheless death reigned from Adam to Moses even over them that had not sinned after the similitude of Adam's transgression, who is the figure of him that was to come.

But not as the offence, so is the free gift. For if through the offence of one many be dead, much more the grace of God, and the gift by grace, which is by one man, Jesus Christ, have abounded unto many. And not as it was my one that sinned, so is the gift: for the judgment was by one to condemnation, but the free gift is of many offences unto justification. For if by on man's offence death reigned by one; much more they which receive abundance of grace and of the gift of righteousness shall reign in life by one, Jesus Christ.)" (Romans 5:12-17)

Now I know that is a lot to digest at one time but it need to be out there so you could actually see it and just maybe it would pop out at you. In the Ark of the Covenant was the tablets that God wrote the Law upon at Mt. Sinai. Many miss the concept about the word of God because of the excuses that holds them back from reading it. Many have excepted Christ and believe in Him but activating the fullness of their salvation they miss because of the deception.

Each individual is given a measure of faith that wants need to be feed, it yearns to be feed, to be strengthen. But what the problem is that we are being feed with the deception of discarding the word of God's protection by tossing the Law of God. The entire word of God is the Law of God. We want to separate it from the Old and the New but Christ brought it to it simplest form. The simplest form stripped the added practices of man and release the divine protection of God. We look at it as the Law God calls it Mercy.

God understood that from the beginning the understanding that we have now they did not have from the beginning. God is pouring out revelation upon revelation upon His people by way of His word. But also we have to remember that the adversary has mixed in and is trying to confuse the people of God with a false message. But the word of God is suppose to be the transforming thing in each us as we read it and study it for ourselves.

The enemy gets such a following because his message message our feelings an emotion but never touch our Spirit because we have not match the word with our Spirit. We have not studied the word for our selves and ask our Lord to give us wisdom and teach us His word. The Bible tells us that the Holy Spirit is the teacher and if that is so them the preacher and the teacher is and conformation oracle.

See when we study and realize that God has revealed something to us then our preachers and teachers confirm it by letting themselves be used as an oracle to have God speak through them about what He is confirming about us. We see the proper order God gives us a call we answer from a measure of faith that He gives us we study His word and reveals to us about us then His true preachers, teachers, pastors are His oracles that confirms what He has revealed.

The Bible records, "My son, keep my words, and lay up my commandments with thee. Keep my commandments, and live; and my law as the apple of thine eye. Bind them upon thy fingers, write them upon the tablet of thine heart." (Proverbs 7:1-3) The Bible also records, "If ye love me keep my commandments." (John 14:15) This is how we confirm that the word has been written on our hearts, that we are carrying the word within us by keeping the word.

Many confuse keeping the word in our heats with memorizing the word but this has nothing to do with it. Memorization has nothing to do with being able to apply the word or understanding the word or keeping the word. To have it written on your heart we know it use it and we follow it and keep it and this is why we study it. This was the reason that the Law was placed into the Ark of the Covenant.

Now the angels and the appearance of the the glory of God I know that it has hit you like a ton of bricks so I not going to spend a lot of time on this. Listen once we are together on the inside and align then heaven must respond. The call went out we answered transformation taking place, position is forming, the Law is being written on our hearts then all of heaven take their rightful position.

The Bible records, "And all the angels stood round about the throne, and about the elders and the four beasts, and fell before the throne on their faces, and worshiped God," (Revelation 7:11)

The Bible also records, "For he shall give his angels charge over thee, to keep thee in all thy ways." (Psalm 92:11) The Bible also records, "And he said, Draw not nigh hither: put off thy shoes from off thy feet, for the place whereon thou standest is holy ground." (Exodus 3:5)

Now as we see these scriptures lay before us we know that God holy host response when the order is correct and holiness is present. God release His angels to supernaturally stand with us as we have spiritually align ourselves with heaven and His glory can fall upon us. We have heard others say to some one, "Wow you look different look like you are glowing." Or we heard, "Look like God is all over you."

So His glory and angels are present when we are align with heaven and once that happen we are exactly what we suppose to be the Glory of God.

Many of us have through away the Old Testament simply because they don't believe it has nothing for us. I want you to know that Christ is there and we have to just study it and see Him there. Once we fine Him then He will lead us to us. The Ark of the Covenant is alive and on the move simply because we the Body of Christ is moving. We are the living tabernacle of God the host of the Holy Spirit, Jesus Christ and our Father.

If we just remember that we are the most precious gift to mankind outside of Jesus Christ then just then maybe we can begin to make a difference in a world that is crying out. The Bible records, "For the earnest expectation of the creature waiteth for the manifestation of the sons of God." (Romans 8:19) Everything and everybody is waiting for the true men and women and children of God to realize who they are and whose they are. Remember my brothers and sisters the Ark of the Covenant is on the Move because you are about your Father's business, Praise Ye the Lord!

Printed in Great Britain
by Amazon